Review of Regulatory Reports

Comptroller's Handbook

Narrative and Procedures - March 1990

Comptroller of the Currency
Administrator of National Banks

Review of Regulatory Reports
(Section 408)

Table of Contents

Review of Regulatory Reports
(Section 408)   Introduction

Each national bank must submit to the Office of the Comptroller of the Currency (OCC) various reports revealing its financial condition or the results of its operations. This information, which is reported for regulatory purposes, is also available for public disclosure to enable investors, depositors, and creditors to better assess the financial condition of the bank. In addition, information from several of those reports is used in the Uniform Bank Performance Report (UBPR) which detects unusual or significant changes in a bank's financial condition as of reporting dates.

This section describes the reports that a national bank must submit to the OCC. The examiner must verify the accuracy of those reports and insist on their being amended if material errors are found. The accuracy of a bank's consolidated reports of condition and income is extremely important because they contain data needed by the computerized-based analysis systems (i.e., UBPR) to detect changing patterns of behavior, not only in individual banks, but also in the entire banking system. If inaccurate data is submitted, the resulting ratios may conceal deteriorating trends in the bank and/or industry.

The examiner assigned "Review of Regulatory Reports" must determine that all reports submitted by management meet statutory and regulatory requirements. Therefore, examiners in each specific department must ascertain from that department's records that the submission of a regulatory report was required and that the report was filed on time, was accurate, and agreed to the bank's general books.

Banks should maintain efficient internal systems and procedures to insure that reporting is accomplished according to the appropriate regulatory requirements. They should develop clear, concise, and orderly working papers to support the compilation of various data. Preparation of proper working papers provides, not only a logical tie between report data and the bank's financial records, but also facilitates accurate reporting and verification.

Preferably, one individual and/or department in the bank should ensure that all reports are filed accurately and on time. All regulatory requests for reports should be routed to that central location. The individual should distribute the request for information to the proper department, coordinate the information obtained, and have the accuracy of the reports checked prior to submission. Ideally, the compilation of the quarterly consolidated reports of condition and income should be verified by means of a procedure instituted by management as a part of the bank's internal audit program. At a minimum, someone other than the person and/or department that prepares the reports should check its accuracy.

A bank's internal control program for regulatory reports should insure that all required reports are submitted on time and are accurate. The specific internal controls employed by a bank to meet those objectives depend largely on the volume of reports, the scope of a bank's operations, and the complexity of its accounting system.

Commonly Required Regulatory Reports

The purpose, form, content, and filing requirements of the most common reports are discussed below. The information contained in these reports, except loans past due 30 through 89 days and still accruing, is available to the public.

- Consolidated Reports of Condition and Income — 12 USC 161(a), 12 USC 1817(a)(3), and 12 CFR 4.11(b)(1) provide that: (1) each national bank submit to the OCC four consolidated reports of condition, including domestic subsidiaries, annually, as of the last day of each calendar quarter; (2) national banks engaged in foreign operations submit to the OCC four consolidated reports of condition, including domestic and foreign subsidiaries, annually, as of the last day of each calendar quarter; and, (3) the OCC can request from a particular national bank, its affiliates, or its foreign branches, special call reports. All national banks receive, prior to the end of each quarter, forms for filing reports of condition. Approximately 20 days after the end of that quarter the Comptroller of the Currency calls for those reports to be submitted within 10 days after the bank receives that request. In addition, the report must be published, in a form that conforms to the official printer's copy provided by the OCC, in a newspaper, published or distributed in the community in which the bank is located, within 20 days of the call date.

  The contents of the call report provide consolidated detailed financial information on assets, liabilities, capital, and loans to executive officers, as well as income, expenses, and changes in capital accounts. This data permits a uniform analysis and comparison for all national banks.

Written instructions for the consolidated report of condition and income will assist the examiner in preparing any balance sheet required in the report of examination. To understand a particular bank's call report, he or she must understand that bank's accounting methods and the information located in, and the relationships between, the bank's general books and subsidiary ledgers. This understanding can only be obtained by a careful review of the working papers supporting each line of the call report and its supplementary schedules.

- Annual Report — 12 CFR 18 allows the majority of national banks flexibility in the preparation and distribution of annual reports. Those banks should notify their shareholders at the same time as the notice of the annual meeting that they may obtain, without charge, basic financial information from the banks. If a shareholder so requests, the bank must provide at a minimum, information substantially similar to that filed with the Comptroller in the reports of income and reports of condition for the two preceding years. However, the format for that information is at the bank's discretion. According to 12 CFR 11, banks whose securities are registered pursuant to the Exchange Act shall furnish to its security holders and to the OCC, annual and quarterly reports, containing similar information.

- Report of Indebtedness of Executive Officers and Principal Shareholders and Their Related Interests to Correspondent Banks — 12 CFR 215 requires that "reporting persons" make a written report by January 31 to the board of directors of their bank if the "reporting person" has outstanding an extension of credit from a correspondent bank of their own bank during the preceding year. The term "correspondent bank" is not all inclusive and is further defined in the regulation. Form FFIEC 004, or a substitute acceptable to the bank, is to be used for reporting those transactions. Submission of those reports will facilitate review of insider transactions by examiners, directors, senior management, auditors, and attorneys.

- Past-Due Loan Reports — The OCC requires all national banks to report the status of past-due loans and nonaccruing past-due loans quarterly as of the last day of each calendar quarter. That report must be forwarded to the OCC as part of the consolidated report of condition and income. The applicable form, Schedule RC-N, sets forth the criteria for determining past-due status. The report facilitates early detection by the OCC of potential loan deterioration and enables it to more efficiently direct the necessary examinations and visitations.

Beginning with the June 30, 1983 call report, individual bank data for past due 90 days or more and still accruing, nonaccrual, and renegotiated "troubled" debt are available to the public upon request. Banks have the option of submitting a narrative statement, not to exceed 100 words or 750 characters setting forth an explanation of the data. The statement appears as submitted on all copies of the report that are released to the public upon request.

- Reports Required by the Monetary Control Act of 1980 — All depository institutions that have transaction accounts or nonpersonal time deposits, that obtain funds from foreign sources, or that maintain foreign branches are required to file weekly or quarterly reports with the Federal Reserve disclosing the level of deposit account balances. Based on the deposit level that each bank reports, the Federal Reserve calculates the amount of reserves that must be maintained at or passed through to a Federal Reserve bank on those deposits. The aggregate reserves required for all depository institutions are used in the formulation and conduct of monetary policy. Rules governing the reserve requirement provisions of the Monetary Control Act are contained in 12 CFR 204. Detailed written instructions for preparation of the required reports are also available.

- Reports Required by the Securities Exchange Act of 1934 — Those reports must be filed if a bank has more than $1 million in assets and a class of equity securities held by 500 or more shareholders. Listed below are the names of the reports, their filing requirements, and their purposes:

  - Form F-1, 12 CFR 11.41—Form for Registration of Securities of a Bank Pursuant to Paragraph 12(g) of the Securities Exchange Act of 1934 ("Exchange Act")—That report must be filed once, not later than 120 days after the end of the fiscal year in which the jurisdictional requirements are met. It is used by the OCC to administer the registration requirements of section 12 of the Exchange Act.

- Form F-2, 12 CFR 11.42—Annual Report of Bank—That report must be filed annually, within 90 days after fiscal year end, or within 30 days of the mailing of the bank's annual report to stockholders, whichever occurs first. It annually updates the F-1 and is used by the OCC to administer, in part, the periodic reporting requirements of the Exchange Act.

- Form F-3, 12 CFR 11.43—Current Report of Bank—That report must be filed within 10 days after the end of every month in which one or more "material" events affecting the bank or its operations occur. The report, in conjunction with other documents in the public file, gives the OCC a current picture of the bank and its operations. It is used by the OCC to administer, in part, the periodic reporting requirements of section 13 of the Exchange Act.

- Form F-4, 12 CFR 11.44—Quarterly Report of a Bank—That report must be filed within 45 days after the end of each of the first three quarters of the fiscal year. In conjunction with other documents in the public file, it gives the OCC a quarterly update, in summary form, of the bank's income, per- share earnings, and general financial condition. It is used by the OCC to administer, in part, the periodic reporting requirements of section 13 of the Exchange Act.

- Form F-5, 12 CFR 11.51—Proxy Statement, Statement Where Management Does Not Solicit Proxies—That report must be filed in advance of any solicitation of proxies or any meeting of shareholders. It must be filed at least 10 days prior to its distribution to shareholders if only the annual election of directors or selection of auditors is to take place. If any other matters are to be voted upon, notices for the meeting must be filed at least 15 days prior to distribution to shareholders.

  Any additional "soliciting material" distributed after the proxy statement must be filed at least 2 business days prior to its distribution to shareholders. Any instructions to solicitors must be filed at least 5 days prior to their dissemination. Any soliciting material, such as speeches, press releases, or radio and television scripts must be filed no later than the date of use or publication.

The bank's annual report to shareholders must be filed not later than the date of distribution to shareholders, or the date preliminary copies of management's proxy statement, in which management does not solicit proxies, are filed with the OCC, whichever date is later. The report is used by the OCC to administer certain reporting requirements of section 14 of the Exchange Act.

– Form F-7, 12 CFR 11.61—Initial Statement of Beneficial Ownership of Securities—That report must be filed by each director, officer, and 10 percent (or more) shareholder. F-7 is reported here only because some banks make a practice of preparing and submitting the F-7 on behalf of the persons affected. It must be filed by or on behalf of the reporting persons within 10 days after that person attains such a position, and it is used by the OCC to administer, in part, section 16 of the Exchange Act relating to insiders' securities transactions.

– Form F-8, 12 CFR 11.62—Statement of Changes in Beneficial Ownership of Securities—That report must be filed by those persons who have previously filed an F-7, if they still maintain an "insider" relationship to the bank. If such relationship has terminated, the filing requirement remains effective for 6 months thereafter. As in the case of the F-7, the F-8 is reported here because some banks prepare and submit the report on behalf of the persons affected. Unless an exemption applies, the document must be filed within 10 days after the end of the month in which any significant change in ownership of securities occurs. It is used by the OCC to administer, in part, section 16 of the Exchange Act relating to insiders' securities transactions.

– Forms F-9A, B, C and D, 12 CFR 11.71—Financial Statements—That report must be filed, in whole or in part, whenever any other form calls for financial statements. It is always used in conjunction with another form and details the format to be followed in the presentation of financial statements. It is used by the OCC to administer, in part, the relevant financial reporting requirements of the Exchange Act.

– Form F-10, 12 CFR 11.46—Form for Registration of Additional Class of Securities Pursuant to Sections 12(b) or 12(g) of the Exchange Act—That report must be filed when an additional class of securities of the bank is to be registered, within 120 days after the end of the fiscal year in which the additional class became "registerable." It supplements that information contained in the F-1 and in all periodic reports filed up to that time. It is used by the OCC to administer, in part, the registration provisions of section 12 of the Exchange Act.

- Form F-12, 12 CFR 11.53—Statement to be Filed Pursuant to Section 11.5(m), Part II—That report must be filed by a bank, if and when it makes a recommendation to its shareholders regarding a pending tender offer. The report is used by the OCC to administer, in part, the reporting requirements of sections 13 and 14 of the Exchange Act.

- Form F-20, 12 CFR 11.45—Amendment of Registration Statement or Periodic Report of Bank—That report must be filed as a "cover sheet" with any amendment to the foregoing documents. The report, containing amendatory material, is used by the OCC to provide a consistent format for amendments to the foregoing documents.

• Lost and Stolen Securities Reporting and Inquiry Requirements — 17 CFR 240.17f-1 provides that every national securities exchange, member thereof, registered securities association, broker, dealer, municipal securities dealer, registered transfer agent, registered clearing agency, participant therein, member of the Federal Reserve System and bank whose deposits are insured by the Federal Deposit Insurance Corporation (reporting institutions) must register with the Securities and Exchange Commission's designee, the Securities Information Center, Inc. (SIC). Each such institution must report lost, missing, stolen, or counterfeit securities to SIC. Each national bank must inquire directly or indirectly of SIC to determine if securities coming into their possession, whether by pledge, transfer, or some other manner, have been reported as missing, stolen, or counterfeit; unless the securities are received from another reporting institution, the issuer or issuing agent, FED in its capacity as fiscal agent, or from a customer, and are registered in that customer's name or its nominee, or in the case of bearer securities when the bank "knows its customer" and can verify through its own records that the securities presented are those that the bank previously sold to the customer. Exempt from inquiry requirements are transactions including bonds with an aggregate par value of $10,000 or less, stocks with an aggregate market value of $10,000 or less, registered securities of the United States government, any agency or instrumentality of the United States government, and securities which have not been assigned CUSIP numbers. All losses, including those under $10,000 must be reported.

- Form X-17F-1A—Form for Reporting Lost, Missing, Stolen, or Counterfeit Securities—That report must be filed with SIC within 1 business day after discovering a theft or loss of any security when: (1) there is a substantial indication of criminal activity; (2) a security has been lost or missing for two business days; and (3) a security is counterfeit. The report must be filed within two business days of notification of nonreceipt when: (1) delivery of securities sent by the bank is made by mail or via draft and payment is not received within 10 business days, and confirmation of non-delivery has been made by the receiving institution; (2) delivery is over the window and no receipt is maintained by the bank; and (3) securities sent by the bank are lost in transit and the certificate number(s) can be determined. The delivery of lost or missing securities to the bank must be reported within 1 business day after discovering and notification of certificate numbers. Securities that are considered lost or missing as a result of counts or verifications must be reported no later than 10 business days after discovery or as soon as certificate numbers can be ascertained. Copies of all reports must also be submitted to the registered transfer agent for the issue being reported and, if criminal activity is suspected, to the Federal Bureau of Investigation.

  Copies of filed or received Form X-17F-1A must be maintained in an easily accessible place for three years.

Transfer Agent and International Activities

Transfer Agent Activities — The reports must be filed if the bank's own stock is subject to the provisions of the Securities Exchange Act of 1934 and the bank is acting as its own transfer agent.

- Form TA-1 (FDIC 6342/01), 12 CFR 9.20—Uniform Form for Registration as a Transfer Agent Pursuant to Section 17A of the Securities Exchange Act of 1934—The form must be filed with the Comptroller of the Currency acting as administering agency for the Securities and Exchange Commission prior to providing transfer agent services involving own bank stock registered under Section 12 of the Exchange Act. Amendments must be filed within 60 calendar days of the date the original information becomes inaccurate, incomplete, or misleading.

- Notice of Failure to Meet Transfer and Processing Time Standards Prescribed by 17 CFR 240.17 Ad-2—The notice must be filed with the Comptroller of the Currency within 10 business days of the end of any month during which the required time standards are not met. The reason for the performance failures, the number of unprocessed items, and planned remedial actions must be included in the notice.

- Notice of Exemption to Transfer and Processing Time Standards Presented in 17 CFR 240.17 Ad-4—The notice must certify receipt of less than 500 items for transfer and processing as registrar during a 6-month period. The certification must be prepared and maintained in the bank's possession within 10 business days of the end of the 6-month period.

- Notice Pursuant to SEC Rule 17 f-2—The notice must be made and kept current to obtain an exemption for classes of persons from the fingerprinting requirements of the above rule. The notice should indicate the duties performed by such classes of persons and describe the bank's procedures to ensure that only fingerprinted employees have direct access to the handling of stocks. The notice shall be kept in an easily accessible place and made available upon request.

International Activities — These reports must be filed if a bank is conducting or intends to conduct international activities through either foreign branches or Edge Act or Agreement corporations. Listed below are the names of the reports, their filing requirements, and their purposes:

- Form CC 7610-01—Notice of International Activity—In accordance with 12 CFR 20, this report must be furnished by a national bank:

  • With a copy of its application to the Board of Governors of the Federal Reserve to establish an initial branch in any foreign country, or any dependency or insular possession in the United States and 30 days prior to the establishment of any additional branches in a foreign country or dependency or insular possession of the U.S. or foreign country.

  • With a copy of its application to the board of Governors of the Federal

Reserve to directly or indirectly acquire a controlling interest in an Edge Act or Agreement corporation or a foreign bank.

- At least 30 days prior to the direct or indirect acquisition of less than a controlling interest in any Edge Act or Agreement corporation or foreign bank, if the cost of such acquisition exceeds $1 million.

This report is used as an analytical tool in determining the soundness of the proposed investments by national banks in foreign countries.

— Form CC 7610-02—Report of International Activity—In accordance with 12 CFR 20, that report is required within 30 days of the occurrence of any of the following international activities:

- The relocation or opening of a branch in a foreign country, or in a dependency or insular possession of the United States.

- The acquisition of any interest in an Edge Act or Agreement corporation or foreign bank.

- The suspension of operations or final closing of any branch in a foreign country, or in a dependency or insular possession of the U.S. or foreign country; or the suspension of operations or final closing of any foreign bank in which a national bank holds an interest.

The purpose of the report is to maintain accurate and current information on the foreign activities of national banks.

— Form FFIEC 030—Foreign Branch Report of Condition—That report must be filed as of December 31 of each year. It details under appropriate headings the assets and liabilities of the branch and provides the OCC with information regarding the types and volume of business conducted at overseas locations. This report also provides information for statistical purposes.

— Form FFIEC 035—Monthly Consolidated Foreign Currency Report—12 CFR 20.5 requires that all banks and banking institutions, including bank holding companies, report exposures in six major currencies if total foreign currency exposure exceeds $100 million. Those monthly reports disclose foreign currency assets, liabilities, and outstanding foreign exchange contracts. Since the reports must be filed on a consolidated basis, the holding company normally will be required to file. Federal branches and agencies are also subject to the requirements but are not required to report data from non-U.S. offices or subsidiaries. The reports provide statistical information and aid bank supervisory agencies in monitoring trading and investment activities.

– Form FFIEC 009—Country Exposure Report—In accordance with 12 USC 161, 12 USC 3906, and 12 CFR 20.10, that report must be submitted by each national bank on a consolidated basis to the OCC quarterly. The report provides statistical information on the distribution by country of the foreign claims held by United States banks and bank holding companies. Portions of the aggregated data are reported to the Bank for International Settlements as part of an international cooperative effort to compile and publish worldwide data on cross-border claims. The report is mandatory for the following national banks and/or bank holding companies, and Edge and/or Agreement Corporations.

- Every national bank in the fifty states of the United States, the District of Columbia, Puerto Rico, and U.S. territories and possessions that meets both of the following criteria:

  – Has at least one of the following:

    - A branch in a foreign country.
    - A subsidiary in a foreign country.
    - An Edge Act or Agreement subsidiary.
    - A branch in Puerto Rico or in any U.S. territory or possession (except that a bank with its head office in Puerto Rico or any U.S. territory or possession need not report if it meets only this criterion).
    - An International Banking Facility (IBF).

  – And has, on a fully consolidated bank basis, total outstanding claims on residents of foreign countries exceeding $30 million.

- Every bank holding company that is required to file the F.R. Y-6 report

(Bank Holding Company Annual Report) and that owns only one bank satisfying the reporting criteria:

– Must file the report on a fully consolidated holding company basis if the subsidiary bank accounts for less than 90 percent of the consolidated holding company's total claims on foreigners. In that case, no report need be filed for the individual bank.

– May file the report, at its option, for either the individual bank on a fully consolidated bank basis, or for the holding company on a fully consolidated bank holding company basis, if the subsidiary bank accounts for 90 percent or more of the consolidated holding company's claims on foreigners.

• Every bank holding company that is required to file the F.R. Y-6 (Bank Holding Company Annual Report) and that owns two or more banks satisfying the reporting criteria:

– Must file a separate report on a consolidated bank basis for each bank that meets the reporting criteria.

– And if the subsidiary banks account for less than 90 percent of the consolidated company's total claims on foreigners, must file a report for the bank holding company on a consolidated holding company basis.

• Every Edge and/or Agreement corporation that has total outstanding claims, exceeding $30 million, on residents of foreign countries, unless it is majority-owned by a bank that must file the Country Exposure Report on a consolidated basis.

• The bank regulatory authorities may specifically require other banking organizations to file this report if the banks are identified as having country exposure deemed large relative to their capital funds.

Other Required Regulatory Reports

The regulatory reports check list summarizes, in addition to the commonly required regulatory reports discussed above, those reports that a bank does not have to file unless a particular event occurs and/or the bank operates a specialized department. The reports are categorized according to the department to which they relate. Although the examiner assigned "Review of Regulatory Reports" must determine that all reports submitted by management meet statutory and regulatory requirements, the examiner assigned to a specific department is responsible for reviewing those reports relating to that department.

Amended Reports

Submission of amended report(s) is required if a material difference is found in the original report. All subsequent reports that are affected significantly by the change must also be refiled, and reports for the current reporting period must be prepared based upon the amended information.

Examiners should use the "Amended Report Notification" form to request amended consolidated reports of condition and income (call reports). Bank management should be instructed to file the amended report within 20 days from the date of request. Any disagreement about the necessity for filing an amended report should be discussed with the supervisory office before completion of the supervisory activity.

Call report amendments must not be submitted on new forms. Rather, a copy of the original report with changes noted in red ink in the margins is preferred. The top right-hand corner of each amended report page should be marked clearly, "Amended." Also, a cover memorandum, signed by the person who prepared the report, and that describes the reasons for the changes, must be attached to the amended report.

The integrity of the data submitted in the reports is vital for effective bank supervision. The report is the only source of financial data used to generate the Uniform Bank Performance Report and the major source for the National Bank Surveillance Video Display System (NBSVDS). In addition, call report data are the key to the Community Bank Scoring System (CBSS) that selects banks for possible off-site analytical review.

The OCC has determined that a "significant error" exists if its correction would result in:

- Changing any amount(s) reported in the report of condition and supporting schedules by more than 1 percent of total assets, provided the amount is greater than $50,000. This criterion must be applied to all supporting schedules of the report of condition.

- Changing any amount(s) reported in the report of income and supporting schedules by:

  - More than 1 percent of total operating income, provided the amount is greater than $5,000;

  - More than $1,000,000; or

  - A material effect on the amount reported as Income Before Income Taxes or on Net Income of the report of income. Examiner judgment should be used to determine whether the change or the aggregate of changes would affect other line items or generated ratios significantly.

The FDIC processes all national bank call reports. Examiners, if they decide it would be useful, may call the FDIC's Call Report Analysis Unit and request a bank's reporting history. The unit may be reached toll free on 800-424-5101 or on 202- 898-6607, Monday through Friday, between 8 a.m. and 5 p.m., Eastern Time. A money penalty referral should be considered against a bank that files significantly inaccurate call reports. (Refer to current policy and procedures for guidelines.) In addition, other enforcement action may be appropriate when reports have significant inaccuracies or are "window dressed."

For annual and other reports, including reports required by the Exchange Act, the OCC has not defined material difference to mean a specific dollar amount as has been done for the consolidated reports of condition and income.

The criteria of what constitutes a material difference depends on the relationship of the difference to the reports in question. The definition of what constitutes a material difference is ultimately decided by a court of law. Presently, materiality has been defined in the following cases as:

- Affiliated Ute Citizens v. United States, 406 U.S. 128, 153- 43 (1972): Facts which "a reasonable investor might have considered important in making of (a) decision (whether to sell)."

- Mills v. Electric Auto-Lite Co., 396 U.S. 375, 384 (1970): Fact "of such a character that it might have been considered important by a reasonable shareholder who was in the process of deciding how to vote."

- SEC v. Texas Gulf Sulphur, 401 F. 2d. 833, 850, (2d Cir. 1968): "Material facts include . . . those which affect the probable future of the company and those which may affect the desire of investors to buy, sell, or hold the company's securities."

- Fiet v. Leasco Data Processing Equip. Corp, 332 F. Supp. 548, 560, 571 (E.D.N.Y. 1971): "A fact is proved to be material when it is more probable than not that a significant number of traders would have wanted to know it before deciding to deal in the security at the time and price in question."

Review of Regulatory Reports
(Section 408)   Examination Procedures

1. Complete or update the Review of Regulatory Reports section of the Internal Control Questionnaire.

2. Determine from review of working papers, the bank's historical record of submitting timely and accurate reports.

3. Obtain a schedule of all regulatory reports filed by the bank since the previous examination. This schedule should include the name of each report and date of filing.

4. Circulate the review of regulatory reports' checklist to those examiners assigned specific departments that generate such reports.

    (The checklist contains an inventory of reports that the bank must submit to the OCC. They are categorized according to the department to which they relate. The examiner assigned to a specific department is responsible only for those reports relating to that department.)

5. Instruct those examiners assigned specific departments which generate regulatory reports to:

    a. Determine from department records what regulatory reports should have been filed because of the passage of time or the occurrence of an event.

    b. Obtain copies of all regulatory reports filed by the department since the previous examination.

    c. Check the reports obtained in b. and the date of filing against statutory and regulatory requirements as shown on the review of regulatory reports' checklist.

    d. Instruct the bank to prepare and submit any delinquent reports.

e. For the most recent filing of those reports submitted on a periodic basis and all other reports submitted since the last examination, perform the following:

- Agree the line shown on the reports to the bank's general ledger, subsidiary ledgers, or daily statements.

- Obtain the bank's working papers applicable to each line item, and agree individual items to the reports.

- Determine whether other examining personnel uncovered any misstatement of assets, liabilities, income, or expense during their examination of the various departments.

- Determine that the reports are prepared in accordance with OCC and/or other applicable instructions.

f. On the basis of the work performed in the preceding step, perform either of the following, as appropriate:

- If the reports are found to be substantially correct, limit the review of the remaining periodic reports filed since the last examination to agreeing major captions to general ledger control accounts.

- If the reports are found to be substantially incorrect, extend the procedures outlined in e. to the remaining periodic reports filed since the last examination for those areas where items were found to be substantially incorrect.

g. Scan all periodic reports for unusual fluctuations. Investigate fluctuations, if any.

h. Complete that portion of the regulatory reports' checklist that is applicable to their department.

6. Retrieve the completed review of regulatory reports' checklist, and:

a. Compare the names of report and dates of filing with the schedule received from management in step 3 and investigate discrepancies, if any.

     b. Review those reports where amendments are required.

     c. Review material differences noted in the annual report.

7.   Review compliance with the missing, lost, counterfeit, or stolen securities requirements of 17 CFR 240.17f-1 by:

     a. Discussing with appropriate officers the procedures in effect regarding the filing of Form X-17F-1A (Missing, Lost, Stolen, Counterfeit Securities Report).

     b. Discussing with the appropriate persons their understanding of the filing, reporting, and inquiry requirements, and by:

        • Substantiating Internal Control questions 6 through 15, as appropriate.

8.   Prepare in appropriate report form, and discuss with management:

     a. Violation of law, rulings, or regulations.

     b. Inaccurate reports and, if applicable, the need for amended reports.

        • If amended reports are requested, complete the "Amended Report Notification" form.

     c. Material differences in the annual report.

     d. Recommended corrective action when policies, practices, or procedures are deficient or when reports have been filed incorrectly, late, or not at all.

The comments must include, if applicable, the name(s) and the "as of" date(s) of amended report(s), the date of filing, amount of, and explanation of, any material difference existing in either the numerical items or narrative statements in the annual report.

9.   Prepare a memorandum, and update the work program with any information that will facilitate future examinations.

Review of Regulatory Reports
(Section 408)   Internal Control Questionnaire

Review the bank's internal controls, policies, practices, and procedures for regulatory reports. The bank's system should be documented in a complete and concise manner and should include, where appropriate, narrative descriptions, flowcharts, copies of forms used, and other pertinent information.

1.   Do requests for all regulatory reports come to one individual or department?

2.   Does that individual or department have the authority to request that required information be prepared by the applicable banking department?

3.   To insure that all regulatory reports are submitted on a timely basis and are accurate, determine:

    a. If completion of the report requires information from several departments:

- Is a written memorandum sent to the various departments requesting the information?

- Is the memorandum addressed to a department head?

- Does the memorandum have a due date?

- Are procedures in effect to send second requests if the memorandum is not returned by its original due date?

- Does completion of the memorandum require two signatures: that of the person gathering the information and that of the person's superior who is held responsible for its accuracy?

    b. If completion of the report requires information from one department, is there separation of duties to insure that the raw data to complete the report is compiled by one person, and verified by another person, prior to submission?

4.   After the report is prepared, but prior to its submission, is it checked by:

    a. The supervisor of the department preparing the report, who takes personal responsibility for its accuracy and submission on a timely basis?

    b. Bank personnel who have no part in the report's preparation?

5.   Do report working papers leave a clear audit trail from the raw data to the finished report, and are they readily available for inspection?

Review the bank's system for compliance with the reporting and inquiry requirements of the lost and stolen securities provisions of 17 CFR 240.17f-1.

6.   Has the bank registered with the Securities Information Center, Inc.?

7.   Are reports submitted within 1 business day of discovery when:

- Theft or loss of a security is believed to have occurred through criminal activity?

- A security has been missing or lost for a period of 2 business days?

- A security is counterfeit?

8.   Are reports submitted by the bank, as a delivering institution, within 2 business days of notification of non- receipt when:

- Delivery is over the window, and no receipt is maintained by the bank?

- Delivery of securities is made by mail or via draft, and payment is not received within 10 business days and confirmation of non-delivery has been made by the receiving institution?

- Securities are lost in transit, and the certificate number(s) can be determined?

9.   Are reports submitted by the bank, as a receiving institution, within 1 business day of discovery and notification of the certificate number(s) when:

- Securities are delivered through a clearing agency, and the delivering institution has supplied the certificate numbers within the required 2 business days after request?

- Securities are delivered over the window, and the delivering institution has a receipt and supplies the certificate number(s) within the required 2 business days after request?

10.   Are securities that are considered to be lost or missing as a result of counts or verifications, reported no later than 10 business days after discovery or as soon after as the certificate number(s) can be ascertained?

11.   Does the bank which functions as a transfer agent make the required reports if it receives notification of loss, theft, or counterfeiting from a non-reporting institution, or if it receives notification other than on Form X-17F-1A, or if the certificate was in its possession at the time of loss?

12.   Are copies of those reports submitted to the registered transfer agent for the issue and, in the case of suspected criminal activity, the Federal Bureau of Investigation?

13.   Are all recoveries of securities reported to the S.I.C., the transfer agent, or the FBI (as appropriate) within one business day of recovery or finding? (Note: Only the institution that initially reported the security as missing can make a recovery report.)

14.   Are inquiries made when the bank takes in any security which is not:

- Received directly from the issuer or issuing agent at issuance?

- Received from another reporting institution or Federal Reserve Bank in its capacity as fiscal agent?

- Received from a bank customer and registered in the name of the customer or nominee, or previously sold to the customer as verified by internal records?

15. Are all reports made on Form X-17F-1A or facsimile?

16. Are copies of Form X-17F-1A and subsequent confirmations and other information received maintained for three years in an easily accessible location?

Review of Regulatory Reports
(Section 408)   Regulatory Reports Checklist

Introduction

The Regulatory Reports Checklist lists the reports/forms a bank must submit. They are categorized according to the department to which they relate.

Explanatory Notes
* = The accuracy of these reports/forms must be verified.
** = The accuracy of these reports/forms need not be verified unless the examiner chooses to do so or unless he/she was instructed to do so by the Washington or District Office.

Instructions

Examiners should ensure that all pertinent reports/forms have been filed and that the filing was done in a timely fashion.

Coordinate your efforts with examiners assigned other areas of the examination procedures to avoid duplication, i.e., Trust, MSRB.

Comments should include, but need not be limited to, the following:

1. For required reports which were not filed or were filed late:

    a. Reason the report should have been filed.
    b. Management's reason for not filing or for filing late.
    c. Date of late filing.

2. For reports containing inaccurate information and/or material differences:

    a. The amount and explanation of the error.
    b. Names and dates of amended reports.
    c. Management's explanation for the error.
    d. Proposed or planned corrective action.

3. For annual report material differences, the amount and explanation of the difference.

Reports of Condition and Income

Every national bank is required to file Consolidated Reports of Condition and Income normally as of the last calendar day of each calendar quarter. These reports provide detailed financial information on assets, liabilities, capital, income and expenses, etc., as of the dates rendered and for the periods covered. The banks must file the following appropriate forms:

Form FFIEC 031—For banks of any size that have domestic and "foreign" offices.

Form FFIEC 032—For banks with assets of $300 million or more without foreign offices.

Form FFIEC 033—For banks with assets of $100 million or more but less than $300 million without foreign offices.

Form FFIEC 034—For banks with assets of less than $100 million without foreign offices.

The previous call reports must be completed and received by the FDIC (or its collection agent) no later than 30 days past the call date, except that banks with more than one foreign office, other than a "shell" branch or an international banking facility, may take an additional 15 days.

The foregoing reports provide consolidated, detailed financial information on assets, liabilities, capital, income and expenses, etc., as of the dates rendered and for the periods covered.

As part of the review of regulatory reports, determine if the balance sheet portion of the report of condition has been published, within 20 days after the call date, in the newspaper in the community in which the bank is located. (12 USC 161)

Detailed instructions and filing criteria are published by the Federal Financial

Institutions Examination Council (FFIEC) in call report instruction booklets. These booklets are designed for banks with assets under $100 million, between $100 million and $300 million, over $300 million, and banks with foreign offices.

Annual Report to Shareholders**

This report is filed annually and provides information specified in 12 CFR 18 on the balance sheet, statement of earnings, reconcilement of capital accounts, and valuation of contingency reserves.

Trust Activities

A checklist for reports that a bank may be required to submit or prepare in connection with its fiduciary powers is provided in Section 1200.802.1 of the Comptroller's Handbook for National Trust Examiners. The checklist includes:

- Trust Reports—General
- Transfer Agent Activities
- Lost and Stolen Securities, 17 CFR 240.17f-1

With the exception of the following reports, the accuracy of the reports listed in the above-mentioned Trust checklist need not be verified unless the examiner chooses to do so or unless he/she was instructed to do so by the Washington or District Office:

Form FFIEC 001*—Annual Report of Trust Assets—This report is filed annually and is used to provide data on trust assets and collective investment funds of insured commercial banks.

Special Report—Fiduciary Activities* (unnumbered)—This report is filed annually by all national banks engaged in fiduciary activities and is used to provide supplemental data on income and expenses and other items for the NBSS Trust Activities Report (TAR).

FFIEC 006*—Annual Report of International Fiduciary Activities—This report is filed annually by banks with overseas units and is used to determine the volume of trust assets overseas. This report should be verified for accuracy only when the overseas unit is being examined; otherwise, the examiner need only verify that it was filed on time.

Form TA-1*—Form for Registration as a Transfer Agent and for Amendment to Registration as a Transfer Agent Pursuant to Section 17A of the Securities and Exchange Act of 1934—The report is filed prior to offering transfer agent services involving registered securities amended as required pursuant to 12 CFR 9.20. It is used to register banks as transfer agents and to facilitate the establishment of a national system for prompt and accurate clearance and settlement of securities transactions.

Form X-17F-1A*—Report for Missing, Lost, Stolen or Counterfeit Securities.

SIC Registration Form* (unnumbered)—Every national bank must register with the Securities Information Center, Inc. (SIC) as either a direct or indirect inquirer for certain securities coming into its possession or control.

International Activities

These reports must be filed if a bank is conducting or intends to conduct international activities either through foreign branches, Edge Act or Agreement corporations.

Form FFIEC 030*—Foreign Branch Report of Condition—This report must be submitted as of the date of the last call in the calendar year. It details, under appropriate headings, the assets and liabilities of the branch, and provides federal banking supervisory agencies with information regarding the types and volume of business conducted at overseas locations. It also provides information for statistical purposes.

Form FFIEC 009*—Country Exposure Report—The report provides data on the distribution by country of the foreign claims held by United States banks and bank holding companies and data on credit extensions that United States banks or bank holding companies grant in foreign countries.

Form FFIEC 019*—Country Exposure Report for Federal Branches—This report provides country exposure information similar to that required from national banks by FFIEC 009.

Form FFIEC 002**—Quarterly Report of Assets and Liabilities of (Federal) Branches and Agencies—Submission of this form is required by 12 USC 161. All federal branches and agencies submit this quarterly report of condition to the local Federal Reserve Bank.

Form FFIEC 035**—Monthly Consolidated Foreign Currency Report—12 CFR 20.5 requires that this report be submitted by all national banks or federal branches whose aggregate foreign currency assets, liabilities, purchases and sales exceed $100 million. The report discloses foreign exchange positions for six major currencies.

Form CC-7610-01**—Notice of International Activity—In accordance with 12 CFR 20, this form must be submitted by a national bank:

- With a copy of the bank's application to the Board of Governors of the Federal Reserve to establish an initial branch in any foreign country, or any dependency or insular possession in the U.S., and 30 days prior to the establishment of any additional branches in a foreign country or dependency or insular possession of the U.S. or foreign country; or,

- With a copy of the bank's application to the Board of Governors of the Federal Reserve to directly or indirectly acquire a controlling interest in an Edge Act or Agreement corporation or foreign bank; or,

- At least 30 days prior to the direct or indirect acquisition of less than a controlling interest in any Edge Act or Agreement corporation of a foreign bank, if the cost of such acquisition exceeds $1 million.

The notice is used as an analytical tool in determining the soundness of the proposed investments by national banks in foreign countries.

Form CC-7610-02**—Report of International Activity—In accordance with 12 CFR 20, this report is required within 30 days of the following international activities:

- The relocation or opening of a branch in a foreign country, or in a dependency or insular possession of the U.S.

- The acquisition of any interest in an Edge Act or Agreement corporation of a foreign bank.

- The suspension of operations or final closing of any branch in a foreign country, or in a dependency or insular possession of the U.S. or foreign country, or the suspension of operations or final closing of any foreign bank in which a national bank holds an interest.

This report is used to maintain accurate and current information on the foreign activities of national banks.

Securities and Corporate Practices

Form F-1**—Form for Registration of Securities of a Bank Pursuant to Section 12(b) or Section 12(g) of the Securities and Exchange Act of 1934 (Exchange Act). (12 CFR 11.290)

This report is filed once, no later than 120 days after the end of the fiscal year in which the jurisdictional requirements are met. The form is placed in a public file for public use. It is used by the OCC to administer the registration requirements of Section 12 of the Exchange Act.

Form F-2**—Form for Annual Report of Bank (12 CFR 11.390)—This form is filed within 90 days after the end of the fiscal year. It serves to update the F-1 annually and is used by the OCC to administer, in part, the periodic reporting requirements of the Exchange Act.

Form F-3*—Form for Current Report of a Bank (12 CFR 11.391)—This form is filed within 10 days of the end of every month in which one or more "material" events affecting the bank or its operations occur. In conjunction with other documents, it gives the OCC a current picture of the bank and its operations. It is used by the OCC to administer, in part, the periodic reporting requirements of Section 13 of the Exchange Act.

Form F-4**—Form for Quarterly Report of a Bank (12 CFR 11.392)—It is filed within 45 days after the end of the first, second, and third quarter of the fiscal year. In conjunction with other documents, it gives the OCC a quarterly update in summary form of the bank's income, per share earnings, and general financial condition. It is used by the OCC to administer, in part, the periodic report requirements of Section 13 of the Exchange Act.

Form F-10**—Form for Registration of Additional Class of Securities of a Bank Under Section 12(b) or (g) of the Securities and Exchange Act of 1934. (12 CFR 11.291)—The form is filed when an additional class of securities of the bank is to be registered and within 120 days after the end of the fiscal year in which the additional class became "registrable." It supplements the information contained in the F-1 and in all periodic reports filed since then. It is used by the OCC to administer, in part, the registration provision of Section 12 of the Exchange Act.

Form F-12**—Solicitation/Recommendation Statement Pursuant to Section 14(d)(4) of the Securities and Exchange Act of 1934. (12 CFR 11.691)—This form is filed by a bank only if and when it makes a recommendation to its shareholders regarding a pending tender offer. It is used by the OCC to administer, in part, the reporting requirements of Sections 13 and 14 of the Exchange Act.

Form F-20*—Form for Amendment to Registration Statement or Periodic Report of Bank. (12 CFR 11.292)—This form is filed as a "cover sheet" with any amendment to the foregoing documents. It is used by the OCC to provide a consistent format for amendments to the foregoing documents.

Financial Statements** (unnumbered) (12 CFR 11.930—11.933)—The financial statements are filed, in whole or in part, whenever any other form calls for financial statements. It is always used in conjunction with another form and details the format to be followed in the presentation of financial statements. It is used by the OCC to administer, in part, the relevant financial reporting requirements of the Exchange Act.

Capital and Related Securities Exchange Act of 1934 Reports

The applicable report(s) must be filed if there are changes, as specified, in the capital structure of the bank. The examiner should keep in mind that when a certificate authorizing the change is issued, the preliminary reports and applications have already been reviewed by the District or Washington office.

Form F-7**—Initial Statement of Beneficial Ownership of Equity Securities to be Filed Under Section 15(a) of the Exchange Act. (12 CFR 11.492)—It is filed by each director, officer and beneficial owner of more than 10 percent of a class of equity securities. It is used by the OCC to administer, in part, Section 16 of the Exchange Act relating to insiders' securities transactions.

NOTE: F-7 is reported here only because some banks prepare and submit the form for affected persons.

Form F-8**—Statement of Changes in Beneficial Ownership of Equity Securities to be Filed Under Section 16(a) of the Exchange Act. (12 CFR 11.493)—The form is filed by persons who have previously filed an F-7, if they still maintain an "insider" relationship to the bank. If the relationship has been terminated, the filing requirement remains effective for 6 months thereafter. Unless an exemption applies, the document must be filed within 10 days after the end of the month in which any significant change in ownership of securities occurs. It is used by the OCC to administer, in part, Section 16 of the Exchange Act relating to insiders' securities transactions.

NOTE: F-8 is reported here only because some banks prepare and submit the form for affected persons.

Notice of Nonpublic Sales and Exchanges** (unnumbered) (12 CFR 16.5(f))—This notice is filed no later than 20 days prior to the time any security is offered or sold in reliance on the exemption provided by Section 16.5 or exchanged for securities of smaller denominations. Used by OCC to determine if a transaction qualifies as a non-public offering under 12 CFR 16.

Form and Content of an Offering Circular of an Existing Bank** (unnumbered) (12 CFR 16.6)—This form is filed by an existing bank in advance of any public offer of its securities. It is distributed by the bank to prospective purchasers of the securities to enable them to make informed decisions concerning the bank and the securities being purchased. Used by the OCC to administer the requirements of 12 CFR 16.

Form and Content of an Offering Circular of a Bank in Organization** (unnumbered) (12 CFR 16.7)—This is filed by a bank in organization in advance of any public offer of its securities. It is distributed by the bank to prospective purchasers of the securities to enable them to make informed decisions concerning the proposed bank and securities being purchased. Used by the OCC to administer the requirements of 12 CFR 16.

Advertisement Statement** (unnumbered) (12 CFR 16.8)—This statement is filed prior to any written advertisement, letter, announcement, film, radio or television broadcast which refers to a present or proposed public offering of securities. It is used by the OCC to prescribe limits on the information that may be contained in the advertisement.

Corporate Activities

In accordance with 12 CFR 5—Rules, Policies and Procedures for Corporate Activities, the OCC decides and acts on filings for structural changes by national banks. (Refer to the Comptroller's Manual for Corporate Activities (Corporate Manual) for sample documents.) Examiners should verify that the appropriate filing was submitted for the following events:

Fiduciary Powers (12 CFR 5.26; Section 10.3 of the Corporate Manual)

Letter of Intent to Exercise Fiduciary Powers** (unnumbered)—The letter should be submitted prior to exercising fiduciary powers. It is reviewed to determine compliance with applicable statutes and regulations to ensure that the bank provides for and retains qualified trust management and to determine that there are no significant supervisory concerns.

Domestic Branches, Seasonal Agencies and Customer-Bank Communication Terminal (CBCT) Branches (12 CFR 5.30-5.31; Sections 11.3 and 12.3 of the Corporate Manual)

Application to Establish a Branch or Seasonal Agency/CBCT** (unnumbered)—This application is submitted whenever a bank wishes to establish a branch or CBCT. It is reviewed to determine compliance with applicable statutes and regulations and that there are no significant supervisory concerns.

Merger, Consolidation, Purchase and Assumption, Corporate Reorganization (12 CFR 5.33; Section 20.3 and 21.3 of the Corporate Manual)

Application to Merge, Consolidate, or Purchase and Assume/Application to Charter an Interim National Bank** (unnumbered)—This application is submitted for approval to merge or consolidate two or more unaffiliated or affiliated operating institutions, to purchase the assets and assume the liabilities of branch offices between commonly owned banks, and to form a one bank holding company. The formation of an interim bank is often necessary to facilitate a corporate organization. It is reviewed to determine the effect of the transaction upon competition, compliance with applicable statutes and regulations, and that there are no significant supervisory concerns.

Amendments to Articles of Association (12 USC 21a; Sections 2.3, 20.3, 21.3 and 30.3 of the Corporate Manual)

Secretary's Certificate, Shareholders' Resolution of Amendments** (unnumbered)—This is submitted when a bank revises one or more of the articles of association. Revised articles are kept in a permanent file as required by law. The secretary's certificate of shareholders' resolutions is used as proper certification of the amendment.

Change in Location (12 CFR 5.40; Section 34.3 of the Corporate Manual)

Application for a Change in Location of Head Office or Branch** (unnumbered)—This application is submitted prior to changing the location of a head office or a domestic (brick and mortar) branch, or a head office to an existing branch site. It is reviewed to determine compliance with applicable statutes and regulations and that there are no significant supervisory concerns.

Letter of Notification of Head Office Relocation to Existing Site and Letter Notifying OCC of Effective Date** (unnumbered)—This letter is submitted to notify the OCC of the effective date of the change in location and is used to update the interagency structure records.

Change of Corporate Title (12 CFR 5.42; Section 36.3 of the Corporate Manual)

Letter of Notification** (unnumbered)—The letter is submitted after a bank changes its title (name) and is used to update interagency structure records.

Operating Subsidiary (12 CFR 5.34; Section 13.3 of the Corporate Manual)

Letter of Notification** (unnumbered)—This letter is submitted when a bank wishes to establish or acquire an operating subsidiary or perform new activities through an existing one. It is reviewed to determine if the proposal raises legal, supervisory, or policy concerns.

Investment in a Bank Service Corporation (12 CFR 5.35; Section 14.3 of the Corporate Manual)

Letter of Notification** (unnumbered)—This letter is submitted when a bank wishes to invest in a bank service corporation. If two or more national banks wish to invest in the same bank service corporation, they may use a single combined notification letter to notify the OCC. It is reviewed to determine if the proposal raises legal or supervisory concerns and that it complies with related laws and regulations.

Change in Bank Control (12 CFR 5.50; Section 31.3 of the Corporate Manual)

Notice of a Change in Bank Control** (unnumbered)—This notice is submitted 60 days prior to the acquisition of a bank when a party wishes to acquire control through purchase, assignment, transfer, pledge, or other disposition of voting stock.

The regulation requires any party acquiring 25 percent or more of a class of voting securities of a national bank to file a Change in Bank Control notice. In addition, if any party acquires 10 percent or more (but less than 25 percent), that party must file the notice if:

- The institution has issued any class of securities subject to the registration requirements of Section 12 of the Securities and Exchange Act of 1934; or,
- Immediately after the transaction, no other party will own a greater proportion of that class of voting securities.

The notice is reviewed to determine that all required information has been provided, that the acquisition does not lessen competition, that the financial capacity of the acquiring party does not threaten the stability of the bank or prejudice the interests of the depositors, and that the competence of bank management is not threatened.

Equity Capital (12 CFR 5.46; Section 32.3 of the Corporate Manual)

Letter of Intent to Change Equity Capital ** (unnumbered)—This letter is submitted when the bank proposes to:

- Issue common stock for other than cash.
- Issue preferred stock.
- Reduce preferred stock.
- Reduce capital by a distribution of cash or assets.
- Reduce par and the sum of capital and capital surplus.
- Change par value of preferred stock.
- Declare a dividend payable in property other than cash.

A Letter of Intent and preliminary approval are not required to issue common stock for cash, reduce par value without changing the sum of capital and capital surplus, or declare a stock dividend.

Any proposed change is reviewed to determine if it conforms to the terms of any capital adequacy agreement; that proposed issuances can be considered capital under the definitions adopted by the OCC; that the change is in compliance with applicable statutes and regulation; and that there are no significant supervisory concerns.

Notification of Change in Capital ** (unnumbered)—This notification is submitted by the bank to report the:

- Issuance of common stock for cash.
- Issuance of common stock for other than cash.
- Issuance of preferred stock.
- Conversion of preferred stock.
- Reduction in common or preferred stock through a distribution of cash or assets.
- Change in par value.
- Declaration of stock dividend or dividend payable in property other than cash.

It is used by the OCC to certify/authorize the change.

Notification of Completion of Reduction in Capital ** (unnumbered)—It is submitted by the bank to report:

- Reduction in par value (not required for stock splits).
- Reduction of common or preferred stock.

It is for the OCC's internal use.

Subordinated Debt as Capital (12 CFR 5.47; Section 33.3 of the Corporate Manual)

Subordinated debt is subject to OCC approval if it is to be considered a part of the bank's capital structure to compute capital adequacy or statutory limitations in accordance with 12 CFR 3.

Letter of Intent to Issue Subordinated Debt** (unnumbered)—This letter is submitted in connection with a proposed issuance of subordinated notes or debentures. It is reviewed to determine the financial impact on the bank, its compliance with applicable statutes and regulations and that there are no significant supervisory concerns.

Notification of Issuance of Subordinated Debt as Capital ** (unnumbered)— The notification is submitted upon completion of the issuance of subordinated notes or debentures to report receipt of funds and certifies that the issue complies with all regulatory and legal requirements, and meets the conditions required by the OCC.

Certificates of Completed Reduction in Outstanding Subordinated Notes or Debentures and Conversion of Subordinated Notes or Debentures ** (unnumbered)—These are submitted to report scheduled reduction or conversions as stipulated by the terms and maturity of the note instrument. It is considered proper certification in reporting a reduction in subordinated notes of a bank.

Letter of Intent to Change Equity Capital ** (unnumbered)—This letter is submitted to notify of the intention to prepay (other than a regularly scheduled payment) subordinated notes or debentures. It is reviewed to determine that it conforms to the terms of any capital adequacy agreement, and that the change complies with laws, regulations and supervisory concerns.

Loan Portfolio Management

Report of Loans Secured by Stock of Other Insured Banks** (unnumbered)— This report should be filed promptly, in letter form, whenever a national bank makes a loan secured, or to be secured, by 25 percent or more of the outstanding voting stock of an insured bank or an insured savings and loan association.

No report need be made when the borrower has been the owner of record of the stock for at least 1 year or the stock is that of a newly organized bank or savings and loan association.

The report is sent to the Board of Governors of the Federal Reserve System, the Federal Deposit Insurance Corporation (FDIC), or the Federal Savings and Loan Insurance Corporation (FSLIC), whichever is applicable.

Deposit Accounts

Abandoned Property Report** (unnumbered)—The frequency of reporting is determined by state statute. The reports are used by states to determine the status of abandoned property held by the bank and the bank's compliance with local escheat laws.

Brokered Deposits** (unnumbered)—The FDIC's regulation 12 CFR 304.6(a)(2) requires prompt filing, in letter form, whenever the total amount of a bank's fully insured brokered deposits and fully insured deposits placed directly by depository institutions as of the end of a calendar quarter exceed either:

- The bank's total capital and reserves, or
- Five percent of its total deposits.

This report must be filed with the FDIC Regional Director within 10 days after the end of such quarter. The report is used to assess the risk these deposits represent to the bank's financial condition.

Due From Banks

Form FR 2900**—Report of Transaction Accounts, Other Deposits and Vault Cash—This form is filed weekly by banks with total deposits of $15 million or more and quarterly by banks with total deposits of less than $15 million. It is used by the Federal Reserve to calculate the level of reserves that must be maintained at or passed through to a Federal Reserve Bank.

Form FR 2950**—Report of Certain Eurocurrency Transactions—This form is filed by every bank that obtains funds from foreign (non-U.S.) sources or that has foreign branches. It is to be submitted weekly by banks with total deposits of $15 million or more and quarterly by banks with total deposits of less than $15 million. It provides information on offshore funds that are used in the U.S. or for the benefit of domestic customers.

Duties and Responsibilities of Directors

Form CC-7029-06a**—Joint Oath of Directors—This form is filed annually by all directors appointed or elected and is used to meet requirements of law.

Form CC-7029-06b**—List of Directors—This form is filed annually by all directors appointed or elected and is used to meet requirements of law.

Form CC-7029-07**—Oath of Directors—This form is filed annually by all directors appointed or elected or immediately after appointment to fill a vacancy and is used to meet requirements of law.